CW00410837

The Real Secret

Dr. Courtney

Robinson

Copyright © 2011 Dr. Courtney Robinson

All rights reserved.

ISBN-10: 1466371145
ISBN-13: 978-1466371149

CONTENTS

1   Dynamic Energy   1

2   Life Source Energy   Pg 6

3   We Are What We Think   Pg 21

4   The Alphabet of Possibilities   Pg 30

5   What Is God?   Pg 39

6   The Race For World Change   Pg 65

7   Clarity   Pg 72

8   Be The Savior   Pg 83

1 DYNAMIC ENERGY

Dynamic energy needs to be brought into the universe and therefore brought into the conscious dimension of the people. We as individuals need to actually breathe life and positive energy into other people and into our communities. So we need to remember that , that it's our dynamic energy that we're bringing forth which raises our vibration to energetically create the phenomenon's that we want to see manifest. We need more energy in our community. There are people that are depressed, that have given up, and that have found excuses not to liven themselves. They have used several reasons why they cannot be completely happy right now, why they cannot be completely fulfilled in the realization of who they are. So we need to become human beings that help them come into their enlightenment and bring dynamic energy, which is the energy that motivates and inspires and moves other people to raise their level of vibration to a higher level. But if we're always looking to others and looking at what they're doing or looking at what they're not doing, then we're not taking advantage of our opportunity to challenge ourselves to bring more dynamic energy into the universe. We should want to bring more energy, to go and tap the well springs of energy inside of ourselves to channel and bring forth more energy into the universe in our own personal life experience, because the quality and the amount of joy and happiness and productivity that we're experiencing in our lives is relative to the amount of energy that we have brought forth from ourselves. So it's a ritual to bring that energy out of ourselves. We say we want to be happier, we want to be healthier, we want to be more motivated, we want to be more positive, we want to be more productive but where does this come from? How can we experience more of this in our lives? What is the source? Is it coming from experiences in the external universe? Is it coming from our ability to respond and our ability to reflect off of what we experience in life? Or is it coming from our ability to internalize what is going on and transmute it and transform it into something that we can use as fuel? So if we want to be happier and more positive and experience a more positive planet, and experience a more positive attitude amongst people, we have to live it and we have to attain it. Because you can be in a positive experience but if you don't have the energy to experience it then what is it? If your energy is not there then we've not accessed it, so we have to challenge ourselves to access more energy. The dynamics of what we call relationships have blinded us from looking at our own energy. Because we have created people and places and things and personalized the energetic phenomenon called us. We have let these people, places and things block us from seeing how our own energy is being projected into the universe. We don't see ourselves; we see the unhappiness that is caused to us by others as though unhappiness comes from outside of us. When happiness comes from inside of you how can unhappiness come from outside of you? It's oxymoronic. You cannot be fully vibrant and operating at your most dynamic level and experience unhappiness in the universe. It's impossible, it's a complete contradiction, but we have gone off into the myths of existence. We live in myths of existence but yet we think that Christianity, Islam, Santa Claus and the Easter bunnies are myths. But each one of us has our own mythological story about what's going on in our lives and why things are the way they are and we believe that it's true. But the way our energy is being circulated has nothing to do with the mythology that we have created to explain our circumstances and situations in life. We are hiding our improper use to radiate and to express the positivity within inside of ourselves; we're hiding that behind these mythological stories of these circumstances that are going on in our lives. We don't realize that it is our perception from the dynamic of being lower energy beings. We're the lower energy beings projected from a lower energy dynamic. If your lungs are clogged how well can you breathe? No matter how much oxygen is in the room, you could have 50 plants but if your sinuses are congested you're not going to be able to breathe. So our energy has been blocked and we refuse to unblock it and to open it up, liberate it and free it because we have become attached to the mythologies of existence. 'This person is doing this and this person is negative and this person is on that and this is because of these people and those people are not doing this and I need this' these are all mythologies of existence. The energy of the most spiritual and high vibrational use of your anatomy, of your physiology, of your biology and of your consciousness has nothing to do with your mythology or your perception of people, situations and circumstances. When you start using this spaceship called your body, and start taking it into higher levels of navigation because you won't be able to travel through atmospheres of higher consciousness if you have not attuned the mechanism that you need to travel to the highest level. It won't even make it into parallel universes of bliss. I'm about to show you how to ascend into parallel universes of bliss.

2 LIFE SOURCE ENERGY

What is a parallel universe? When we're thinking of parallel universes we're thinking about shooting out into space somewhere and into some type of other galactic plane, right? But I'm telling you that we now exist in a field where there are multi-dimensional parallel universes all existing at once, and we are only experiencing one that is consistent with our mythology about existence. We think that it is a reality, that our attachments to this, them, they and those circumstances, we think that that is reality, but it's not. It's something that we have made up and called a life story. A story that we keep going on where we only pick out certain details that are relevant to validate the story that we are attached to. A billion things have happened to us in all the different type of relationships that we have interfaced in. Billions of things have happened. We've only picked out certain details that we call 'our life story', and the reason why we are the way we are and our situation is the way that it is. Now another perception can walk in your exact same footsteps and walk the exact path that you did and pull out a whole different story. Out of your same exact circumstances they would highlight different details that would create a different myth about what is really going on and what is really happening. They would put your shoes on, walk your whole life the way you do and they would pick out different details and come up with another story. That's how fake the story is, and that's how we can shape it out of the events and occurrences that go on in our life. We can shape out these stories. I want to take us beyond the stories, beyond the mythologies of our life and put us back into the energetic driver's seat, because if your energy is high then you're going to start creating more of a positive story. You're going to start highlighting things in your life that make the story better, that creates an open-ended story that seems like it has a positive overview. You are going to start to create a happily ever after story because of the vibration that you ascend to once we realize that we are energy. We are not the bodies, the circumstances or the situations that we are. We are energy, and as we project more of ourselves because when I say energy, energy is God, energy is the divine, energy is the source, and energy is consciousness. When we use these vehicles to channel more of our powerful energy into the universe things change in the universe. We begin to push through barriers of dense circumstances. We have what I call second wind experiences where you give up, you've got to that exhausted point in your day and you're tired of this, that and the other. But then when you go in and channel more energy, because the myth is 'that I've done too much, I've been doing all of this all this time and I've been doing this and I'm this, that and the other and I'm 40 years old, I'm 50 years old, I'm 21 years old and all these years'. This is all myth; it has no relevance or significance to the amount of energy that you contain as a divine entity. But we slow down responding to the myth. The myth of age, the myth of height, the myth of width, the myth of strength, the myth of health, these are myths that we have programmed ourselves to respond to and to believe in. So we say, using nutrition as an example, 'I need this much food to eat, I haven't eaten enough today, I don't have energy' mythology! A person will skip or eat a meal every other day and have more energy than people who claim they have nutrition. It's not real, it's mythological, it's a fable, but if they realized themselves as energy they could channel and harness and bring forth more of the energy that is them into the universe. We have become vampires on a physical plane, lower level vampires, let me show you how, because if you don't realize the energy that is you then you would have to prey off of lower level situations to get energy. People think that they are getting energy from their food but we can give food to a dead body, it's not going to get up. So life force energy or life source energy is the highest quality of energy that one can gain right? Because that's what we used and what we have to come into this planet; life force energy. That doesn't come from the food. If it did then we could give a dead body carrot juice right? And it would get up wouldn't it? Because there's life force energy in it, correct? We could make a salad and go down to the cemetery and give a salad to a dead body and it would get up right? Is that gonna happen? No, because there is no life force energy in the body so it's not going to get up even if we fed it with salad and carrot juice. So if that's not the life giving element, if the life giving element is not in the material universe, where is it then? Where is it coming from every day when you get up in the morning? It's not coming from your breakfast because you get up before you eat breakfast. Where is it coming from? And how do we get more of it to maximize more of our energy and our potential? And to use more of our brain and take advantage of more of the time in the day to create and manifest, how do we do it? Not from food. Got a person saying 'I'm going to eat super nutritious, high level food with all of this energy in it but I still don't feel like working out. I'm tired; I don't feel like doing any God damn push-ups. I don't feel like running and jogging and doing anything really' but you've got this high level of nutrition from the food though right? You should be overwhelmed with the energy from the food because you are eating the highest quality of food. You had the highest quality of food that day; the food you ate was all organic but you organically don't wanna do a God damn thing organically. You are organically lazy. Then you eat more thinking that you need more energy, you eat more organic stuff, and now you're organically fat. You're even chewing organic and you still don't wanna do anything else. You don't have any ambition, any focus, you can't start a task and finish it from beginning to end, what's the problem? You've got the best food right? On days that we eat organic food we should be able to do laps around the planet, and around meat eater's right? What's the problem? What's going on? We can overdose on the nutrition but what's the effect that we're going to get if we overdose on nutrition? Are we gonna have more energy, all this radiant energy? Mythology! You're not going to have more until you go in those moments and choose to have more energy. When you go within, to the well springs of power within yourself in those moments and choose to push forward like a woman in labor. You're pushing more energy out as you, 'I'm not gonna stop now'. You're breaking through and your expanders are getting bigger. Your capacity to hold energy is growing so tomorrow you have what you pushed forth from yesterday. This is how we get more powerful. We keep channeling our energy, pushing it further past the resistance of the material world. The material world is dense; the laziest people can't push the life force energy of themselves through the density of the material world. It's so dense that they just want to sit down at home all day and do nothing. They're intimidated, and it is not a physical density in the sense of that they're physically lazy, it's a mental density where even the smallest thing will be too much. 'Well I just need you to pick up 500 pieces of lent'. 'It's too dense, I can't do it! I won't do it!' 'I can't do it!' 500 pieces of lent is nothing, its light, am I correct? But even if we said pick it up one by one the density of the material plane, the gravity of thought and consciousness weighs so heavy. They say 'I can't do it, I'm not picking up the 500 pieces of lent, and I can't pick up the 500 pieces of lent'. We come back, the 500 pieces of lent are there. When we become more dynamic and more energetic, more alive and generate more vitality in ourselves then we help push people past their energetic blockages by them just even being in our presence. Because we are so fired up we're like 'yes you can!' 'You can push through that, you can make it through that, yes you can do that, your energy can rise above that, you can put that energy forth, go ahead you can make that, you can handle that'. So we're motivating them because we're sharing the dynamic force of our energy with them. But our ability to motivate more people and larger amounts of people down to our entire community will require that we bring more energy from within ourselves, more chi, more prana, and more life force into the planet. Because now you have to motivate all these people, we have to share our energy to move them past the blockages to get their energy spinning. How do we do that? Some say nutrition; it's what you eat. No, it's not what you eat. If you eat nothing or a little you can still bring dynamic energy out of yourself. It's about your will power; what you will to do and what you realize. If we stay focused and know that the energy is inside of us, we can challenge ourselves to bring more of it out at each and every moment of our existence. And when we challenge our myths about how we perceive the day and I wanna go deep here because we've got a myth about how the day is going, what people think, how they feel, 'everybody seems mad today, everybody seems depressed today, everybody seems like they don't wanna do anything, everything is working against me', myth! At those moments push your energy further. That's the myth talking because energy has no myth. It's raw; it has no perceptual framework it takes us to perceive it. It's just energy in motion ready to be utilized and directed by those who realize themselves as the directors, and those who realize that they're in the driver's seat at that moment. So we've got to realize when we have chosen a defeatist myth about things. And they call that a defeatist attitude; where you have given up before you have even got started. You've given up and you think that the circumstances are real. But the circumstances are relative to the matter of energy that you're willing to put forth. Because if you put more energy forth you find yourself saying 'Well I could have done that anyway that was nothing. Wow! I made it through that' but the myth that's relative to the lack of desire to put out more energy seems like the total reality.

'We aren't gonna be able to do this, this is this, that and the other' then you get the negative mind with the negative thoughts which are mythological thoughts. The whole negative thinking process of how the mind works is all myth and it is really just energy that does not see itself. It actually believes that it is limited to the myth that it has created. When it sees its source, then it pushes forward and produces more. If it doesn't see its source then it just generates the myth. The myth will be the present circumstances that it believes that it cannot go beyond. But once it says 'Wait a minute, let me just put more of myself out' then the illusion of what the dense circumstances are, are dissolved, and we ascend to a higher level in those moments. That means we have to have moments of ascension. If we're not having moments of ascension every day something is wrong. That means we think we've reached a limit of what we can do, be and have and once we reach that limit we ascend beyond that perception by putting more energy forth. 'I've reached my limit, I've got to stop, this is it, it's like I'm doing everything' ascension moment, 'I'm gonna do more', lol! 'That's about it for the day, I don't have this or that and I need these circumstances to change which are currently not working my way, this is not going like I wanted it to' all mythology, ascension moment, because we will not get past those circumstances until we become the navigators and skyrocket beyond the illusion of these circumstances. They are not going anywhere until we bring more energy into the universe. Our life is not going to change in any way until we bring more energy into the earth. Our community is not going to change until we as a people bring out more energy for transformation. If we don't bring the energy out, guess what? It's going to look the same as it did yesterday. It is going to reach the level of our capacity to bring dynamic energy into the planet. We say we want more but we think of that as capitalistic. We want more money, we want more people, we want more material. We think that once we get more of these things that then we will get more of something else, but do you know what we really are asking and what we really need? It's more energy. You put more dynamic energy into this plane from within yourself we propel all these things in motion to happen in our life. We want more people around us, then we need what? More energy to dialogue with them, right? More energy to connect with them, more energy to propel them further, am I right? Or how are they going to show up? We don't have enough energy to make it through the density of those of whom we are in association with so how are we then going to create world change? We are not going to create world change until we can become so animated and so energized that we can bring the quality of energy into this planet that moves the whole thing into a different direction. Wherever we see world change we see beings of great energy fields. These beings had great energy coming from them to move, motivate and animate this planet to create eras. So much energy that their existence during that particular time created a whole new era based on a change that they caused. What am I saying? We've got to become more energized. We don't get more by wanting more we get more by tapping into more energy at times when it's most relevant for us to ascend to greater levels of experience. We need more dynamic energy. We've got to go beyond giving up, go beyond our perception of limits which are myth, go beyond the type of co-dependencies that limit us from what we can achieve. That's the same thing as saying 'because somebody else is negative, because them, those and they are negative then I have to be' But when you say 'No, my job here is to bring higher energy', more energy into this planet to attune my frequency to master channeling energy through this vehicle called this human body, there's no co-dependency in that state. Because whatever anybody is doing you're challenging yourself to bring more energy forth out of you because whatever you don't use you lose and whatever you master you get more of it. So this does not necessarily have a lot to do with anybody else because if the energy you're putting out is only at 0.2% then no matter what anybody else does, your capacity is 0.2%. And you can get with some other people and travel around the world and guess what? You're at 0.2% wherever you go. So stop being distracted by anybody and anything that anybody is doing and take your percentage and take your energy to 100,000%. Because now that's what you have to attract, magnetize, affect and to move forth, period. People don't understand that spiritual energy can be transferred even through technology, but the quality must be high so that when people on the other side of it experience it, they're impacted and mobilized and charged up to make superior moves. But that means in order to do that more energy must be brought forth. We have to become much more energized. We cannot be lackadaisical, lethargical, depressed and passive. And we cannot have myths that make us prone to other people's negative attitudes. We've got myths that do that. There's a few myths running that say 'I'm affected by what other people do' but when you came out of your mother's womb if you didn't have the energy to breathe to make your lungs move, you would have died. What did that have to do with you being attached or related to anyone on this earth? If you didn't have that dynamic energy at the point of birth, you would have died on a personal level. So the quality of your personal life is relative to the dynamic energy that you can manifest at any moment of time. There were no friends or social groups when you came out of the womb, was there? And if you didn't breathe and cough past the mucus in your lungs, or find the dynamic energy to push past the density of the mucus in your lungs, you would have died. What do you think is different now? The only difference is at that point we were not distracted, we knew that life was relative to us putting more of our energy into the physical body to exist. Now, we're distracted by social groups, religious ideologies and mythologies. We are distracted from channeling our own energy into the planet to create.

3 WE ARE WHAT WE THINK

What if I put it this way, that we are self-sustained beings. Some people say 'I wanna be a futilitarian', 'I wanna be a breatharian', 'I wanna be a vegetarian', but all that's secondary. We are self-atarians and if we put low level energy into the planet for us to live off of, we have no energy to move with, no matter how much we eat. It's how much life force we allow to seep out can we live off of. How is this life force coming out? Through thought, we project higher levels of thoughts. This whole entity is motivated by higher level thought to move into action. This entity we call self, called the body is motivated by higher level of thought. Thought is the food, consciousness is the food. Give you an example, you think a sexual thought, you're aroused and motivated, no nutrition. Just a sexual thought in and of itself you're stimulated and motivated right? Where was the nutrition at? You actually propelled yourself into existence by thinking a particular type of thought. You got energy from nowhere, dynamic energy. You project a negative thought, you depress yourself, and you have no energy. We are feeding our own selves through our thought food. We are not what we eat, we're what we think. We are what we think constantly and continuously and perpetually. And if we're perpetually thinking low level vibrations of thoughts, thoughts of attachment and dependency on the material universe then we are at the densest level of existence. We've got to start living in higher thought realms and we will start to ascend to higher experiential realms because thoughts are things, and when we're thinking on a higher level the quality of things transform in our life. This is a reality. If we want something higher we don't get it by wrestling with the material world, we get it by ascending in thought, and breaking through illusions. Everything is here right now. We have a billion dollars right now; we have a trillion dollars right now. Do you know why we don't see it? Because we have accepted a mythology that it isn't there and we believe that it's not there. But all is there. In the quantum realm and the quantum reality everything is here. The only reason we don't see it is because of our perception and when we raise our thought levels to be able to perceive it, it manifests instantaneously as though it was always there. So our experience of not having is a mythological creation that we continue to perpetuate. We're perpetuating not having and seeing not having when everything is there. Why is everything there? Because at the sub-atomic level everything is made of the same thing so if everything is made of the same thing everything is in everything and could be anything. What makes it what it is? Our consciousness. It molds, shapes and fit's the form of our consciousness at the speed of thought. It's simultaneous with the speed of our thoughts. We speed up our thinking; higher quality thoughts we will begin to see something else. Go back over your day; everything you saw was a lie. Play back every negative thought; lie, lie, lie, lol! Every negative thought you had was a lie but it was your myth and your story that you acted out and played out. But at the point that you realize that it was a lie now you can go beyond it, you've just transcended it. But some people are attached to thought. If only they knew that they were going to need to bring more dynamic energy out of themselves by knowing that the self is the source then they wouldn't be attached to thought. We live in a self -generated universe, and we are the self-generators and everything that we're experiencing we are generating. We must turn up the generators. We think that what is being generated is real; I'm trying to take us to the generation button and turn that up. Nothing that we are experiencing is real, it's as real as we perpetuate it. Project something else and there will be something else. When we say we are God and we are God consciousness, what do we mean? It's not a historical concept; this is a concept of who we are in essence and how we relate to the experiences that we are having. We're not saying we're God because we mimic or we look like those of ancient. But when you say you're God you're saying that you are the consciousness that has generated all that is. All that is has always been, we generate the experience of what it is. We're the movement of it. We're when and how and what it becomes and what it means. We're the generators, the operators and the destroyers of illusions. We create realities. Some of us get lost in the illusions; the Mayas when we believe the myths we created are the absolute truth. We go to the movies and we are crying in the movie. We are upset in the movie. We hear gunshots on the screen we're ducking in the movie, we throw our popcorn on the ground and we're running out of the movie theatre. It's a movie! We're constantly writing the scripts but if we want to become better script writers, we're going to need more fuel to burn overnight so that we've got all of the energy we need to write the perfect script. The scripts that we're writing are some low level scripts. We are writing some low level, low budget scripts, lol! And that's all the drama and the conflicts that we are experiencing, it's a low level damn script. 'I'm writing that person is mad, that person is upset and that person doesn't accept what I want, and that person is hating on me', that's what you're writing. You are writing that. We are writing these things. Write something else, take your most negative thought and then just erase it and write something else. You will be surprised and I know that sounds crazy but your most negative thought that you think is reality is really mythology. It's mythology. Why is that so if I ask you 'Why is that the definite truth of things?' You will say 'because it is'. Why? Because you have it to be so and you will not have it any other way, that's the real reason. If you decide to have it another way then you have become open minded, and the light bulb comes on and you get an epiphany and you say 'Well what is that? What about that? It could, well since you put it that way' Now you're learning. That's knowledge.

We call knowledge old information. We have called stories knowledge. That's not knowledge. What you already know is no longer knowledge anymore. Everything that you know is not knowledge anymore. Everything you know is ignorance. Because if everything you knew was knowledge then why would you need to know anything else? Because everything you find out will make what you thought you knew ignorance. Everything you know is ignorance and the fact that you believe that it is knowledge is mythology. Look at the stuff that our parents told us when we asked them questions. They gave us good answers but as we studied more we realized how ignorant those answers were. 'Why is the Sun up there?' 'Because God created it'. 'Oh, OK I guess that answers it'. And we say 'Well I've got the knowledge of why the Sun is created'. But then when somebody says 'No, that actually all these cosmic situations happened and there's energies and gasses in the universe that are merging together' then you say 'Wow! I was ignorant'. So what was knowledge became ignorance. We can speed the process up, everything that you think you know about anything you're ignorant about it, and do you know what your greatest ignorance is? You don't know that you're generating it. We're looking for truth but we are generators of truth. The seer is the truth that they see. No seer no truth. Get rid of the seer and where is truth at? The seer and truth are inseparable. We are the truth, we generate truth. Our direct experience of reality is our truth. But do you know what the lie is about that truth? It's not all encompassing. So since it's only a truth, our truth and the truth for the moment subject to change based on more awareness then it is a lie. It is not truth, it becomes relative. Only non-relativity is truth. Everything relative is partially true and partially a lie. If you can see the partial lie of it, now you are awakened to the bigger picture. Not by having another truth but seeing the partiality of the truth that you have is your very awareness of the greater truth. Not polarization, 'I've got a truth, let me find the truth'. If you find another truth you find another lie. But when you know that the truth that you have is only part of the all, only a certain dimension of the all that is, now you are in touch and in tune with the greater truth. You are aware of it, you do not possess it, you do not have it but you are in tune with it. People come and they say that 'My truth is the truth', they have imprisoned themselves, that's a prison that you cannot get out of. Then you say to them 'you know what; you can get out of jail, you can just walk right out' 'No I can't! I can't just get out of here.' You have imprisoned yourself in a truth because you refuse to see the unlimited possibility that lies within the all. So what we think are our truths that we fight for, are our prisons. And someone comes and liberates you from the prison, you really want to get out but you are so attached to your truth, your myth, the part you have been playing for so long. It's the role or the part that you have been playing for so long; you don't wanna give up that part. You were Eddie Murphy in Trading Places; the poor version and you didn't want to change your role to 'Coming to America', lol! Same damn actor, different role. You thought the movie that you had before or the myth that you had before was your life so you fight for that 'No, this is who I am' somebody says 'No, there's infinite possibility that's who you have been'. Everything you think you were or everything you think you are is old. The person that you thought you were has already died you don't have to worry about them anymore. But we're fighting to keep the illusion of them going. Change is the only thing constant but we fight for the myths while we attract information contrary to what we believe. Our ego gets inflamed because we attract information contrary to what we believe, our ego is flared up 'I know this, I know this, I know that' but why did you attract the information? To open yourself up to more than your part. To open yourself up to the total spectrum of what's possible. So it's not who has the truth, it's how open am I to the total perspective of what is possible. We think it's a battle of truth versus truth, this truth versus our truth versus my truth versus their truth. No! It's the reality of multiple truths and the option of what to create. Wow! Now we have escaped out of the prison and whatever truth that we have temporarily we wear it like loose clothes. 'They do for now'. But if we find something higher and something greater to manifest the dynamic reality of a higher and more splendid vision, then we take those loose clothes off and put on something else. But the people who are attached say 'No! These are my clothes' 'But you've been wearing them for two years! We've got silks and linens', but they still respond by saying 'These are my clothes'.

4 THE ALPHABET OF POSSIBILITIES

So I'm saying that we've got to go beyond the myths, we've got to go beyond mythological consciousness. That's how we've got duplicate religions; Christianity, Judaism and Islam because we are looking for any myth. So it's not just an attack on religious ideology, it's an attack on the childlike, mythological mind of the immature, unspiritually developed individual, because any myth will do. And not just myths in the sense of parables and ancient stories but just any old myth. We live in several myths and that's what the matrix is; a mythological world where things are not real and are not what they seem to be. There's something there but the limits of what it could be are not perceived. The unlimited nature of it we're unaware of it. That's myth and mythical mindedness. When you go beyond the myth, you see the symbolic nature of things of how they point to the bigger picture but don't really represent it so that you're not trapped. We've got to go beyond the myths, the myth called us, what we're capable of doing and what we're not capable of doing. When I say 'Figure things out' look at the words, 'figuring out', you're getting out of something. Out of a box, a construct and out of a paradigm, 'let me figure this out'. You're figuring yourself out of a limited paradigm or perception of reality. That's how we get liberated. But in the realm of attachment people have a right to create limitation for themselves and they do it all the time. But if they want something more then they have to be willing to let those limitations go to have another experience, and it may be completely unorthodox and completely beyond what they could have imagined. How do you go beyond your imagination? Give it up, lol! You want to go beyond imagination, give up imagination, and give up what we have imagined. What are some of the things we have imagined? That Jesus Christ came out of the sky and mother Mary had him and he's gonna come back on the clouds, that's imagination. If we want to truly go beyond imagination we need to give it up. Give up all the things that we are imagining. You know the things that we are imagining? Situations that have not concluded and we already have the conclusions for them. If it has not concluded and you have a conclusion can you realize that you are in a realm of imagination right now? That you are fascinated so much with imagination that you have concluded everything that's going on without no end? It's not over with so any conclusion that you have come to is purely imagination. How many circumstances are we experiencing through imagination? Let me show you the quantum aspect of the universe. You have A through Z that could happen and there are more letters than that, fathom that, but you have A through Z of all the possibilities that can happen. You pick Y possibility and you stick on that one. And you're getting all into imagination when you experience Y happening right now completely. You are clear that Y is the ultimate result. But you have a whole alphabet of possibilities; all the way through A to Z, and nothing has happened but you are set on Y, that's imagination. We are not even present. At each and every moment we should re-presence ourselves to infinite possibility because if we open ourselves up to infinite possibility we know it's not just Y, it just might be U, lol! It just might be I, it could be C, and it might be what you want it to B, lol! But you're stuck on Y, that's what you're stuck on and that's your imagination. And if you could go beyond that you could C that what you want can B and that is U and that is I, lol! And I know that it's funny but it's deep. So we've got to alter our consciousness in every moment, we're talking about waking up the world but we cannot alter our consciousness moment to moment. We have become fatalistic, we're saying 'it's over with' with each and every negative perception that we get. We can't watch the mind and see negative perception but we claim that we are meditators, but we can't see negative perception. We can't see our reaction to negative perception and our creation of the things that we don't want to happen through our reaction to negative perception, but we are going to change the world. And the world we are trying to change we are creating it by reacting to our imagination. The world we are trying to change doesn't even exist and the world that we want to be is relative to what we are willing to do. The world we are trying to change does not exist, that world is a world of myth. And what the world really is; is liquid, ready for us to crystalize it into magnificent shapes. It's like an experiment a quantum physician did. He spoke letters to water and then froze it, and then he went and got a microscope and looked at the different crystal formations that the water took on due to the different words that he spoke to it. So the water had no real molecular structure of its own, it was relative to the energy that he put into it. That's what the universe is, it's nothing. It's nothing and everything you want it to be at the same time. Wow! The question we begin to ask is what are we energetically prepared to want it to be? How much are we able to channel our awareness in each and every moment of our experience to guide its creation process to the divine result that we want to manifest? That's what it boils down to. So this is not just another good book, this should be taken into our awareness into each and every aspect of our day. Nothing and nobody is real and the only reality that you will experience is one relative to the state of energy and vibration that you're in.

Yesterday is over with but many of us will get up
tomorrow and believe that the myth of yesterday has
some effect over today or over the next day. So we react
today as though it is yesterday but tomorrow has already
forgotten in the flexible liquid memory of the universe.
The universe has no memory but when we get attached to
thoughts it becomes very mindful. So yesterday is over
with, dead and gone. No one that was here yesterday
existed because that projection of themselves was an
illusion and it was not who they are. So if yesterday was
not who they are then what is it? It is an illusion. They all
could be something else, dynamically different, radically
different. Do you know what determines it? How
radically different we are and the quality of energy that
we put forth. I think we should start putting all of our
negative energy forward, looking at it, and projecting it
all from ourselves. See all the negative circumstances that
we have really reacted to, that we are making up. Let it all
play out in your mind, this is what I call a mental
cleansing, and then react to life the opposite of how you
would react to the myth of all the negativity. Because
you're creating it when you react to it as though it is real

but when you watch it and react opposite to that, you see how much of an illusion that myth is about how things really are. You say 'well, blah, blah, blah somebody doesn't even like me, they don't like me, that person hates me, that person doesn't get along with me, that person doesn't accept what I have to offer, that person is not open', vent all that out and then act towards that person the opposite of the myth that you believe. You will see magic. You'll see how you do not have to react to the illusions of old thought patterns and thought streams. That you have a choice, that you're not a pattern of streams of thoughts, and that you are the thinker. Streams of thought pass through our minds and we act as though it's us which is why we never create what we want. We don't realize that everything that flows through your mind is optional. That's why people are in mental institutions because they don't know that what's going through their mind is optional. They actually think that's what it is, 'I heard a voice and it told me that's what it is'. No, that was just a stream of thoughts you had. They can't separate the thinker from patterns of thoughts that are either in the open psychic field of the universe or just their own genetic material from their DNA of their parents and their ancestry just vibrating on. They can't separate the thinker from that. What's the difference between the thinker and the thoughts? The thinker is the chooser the thoughts are the options. That's the only difference. You go to a store feeling hungry; the thought is to buy everything right? You want everything you see. These are all your options of what you can eat. The thinker says 'No, we don't need to get 5 different packs of cookies' because you have separated the stream of a pattern of thoughts from the thinker in that very moment. You could have said that 'The desire for cookies have taken over me because I'm hungry. I'm gonna need chocolate chip cookies plus oriole cookies plus peanut butter cookies' that's three different cookies. Instead you said 'No, I don't need that, I only just need to get one' but the thought of all of it hits you 'I could eat all of this right now'. That's what they mean when they say that your eyes are bigger than your stomach. Your consciousness is spewing out more thoughts than is necessary for you to create or manifest. So when the thinker separates himself from the thoughts, that's when you become God awakened because God chooses, God creates.

5 WHAT IS GOD?

God is not the by-product of patterns that have been
streaming on this Earth from the beginning of time. What
do I mean? There are energy fields on this plane that we
can affect or be affected by. Every atmosphere has an
aura, energy and a vibration of its own. And if you walk
into the aura, energy and vibration of that atmosphere
you will receive thoughts. Many people are at a
reactionary level of thought fields in atmospheres. This is
where they exist at. They go into rooms and energy fields
are already there. Matter is living; all matter has thoughts
and stored thoughts. Everything in the universe stores

information and memory. Everything in the material world stores memory in consciousness. When we go into the fields of these material realms, we pick up on the thoughts. This planet had a thought before we got here and we can either come with the dynamic energy to move the thoughts along, to stir them up and move them in the direction of what we're creating or we can be open to the thoughts that are already here. There were thoughts already here about what black people are for example, and they were just spewing out in the universe as patterns 'Black people are this, black people are that and black people are this' and many people owned it. 'Black people are Negroes, black people are this, black people are that' and then consciousness manifested on this planet and said 'Black people are great'. That means it ascended beyond the field of old collective thought energy just travelling in the universe about who we are. Many don't go beyond that they just go and accept it. They read the history books and they just deal with the fields of old thoughts and old information. The ideas of dead people that are just travelling around, thoughts of George Washington and Abraham Lincoln just stuck on this Earth, dense energy.

Many people incarnate on the planet and they are just open to the psychic field of what's there. And then when a God is born; that's an entity that is not limited to the psychic field of this plane. That's one that can come here and create. That ascends beyond the density and the limited amount of thoughts that are circulating and then creates a new perception. That is what God consciousness is; that which can give birth to new perception on the material world. We think God is a being that is somewhere in the sky sitting on the planet on a throne. We think God is some entity that existed somehow at the beginning of time and has disappeared until the end. We don't realize that God is just that which gives birth to new perception; the creator. But if everything was already there in the universe, what the hell did God create? A new perception of it. Everything was already there because God is the all, isn't he? So what did he create if he is everything? He had to create something that was non-material; perception. He created different perception of everything and here we are. Because even though the whole material universe is complete, it can still be perceived in one billion, trillion, infinite different ways.

The creator is that which perceives everything differently. Wood was already there, perceive it differently it's a table. Perceive it differently it's a door, perceive it differently it's a pencil and it goes on forever but there is no more or less material in the universe. The all is complete, all is all, there will never be any more all or in the all but do you know what? It's constantly being perceived differently and perceiving itself differently. Because while the realm of material is solid and this is a paradox, the realm of material is solid; complete and full, the realm of perception is infinite. That means that while a room appears to be completely and absolutely totally what it is we can come up with billions of different perceptions of it and experience it in one billion different ways. So while the room is completely something solid, our perception is the realm of infinity that overlays the material world. Matter is already there, it's already solid but matter doesn't experience itself consciousness experiences matter. Matter experiences itself through consciousness. Matter; the material world is self-conscious through the mind of man and woman. We are how matter becomes conscious of itself, without us, matter would not even matter, lol! So the God at the beginning of the universe was the great perceiver. When is the beginning of a universe? Let me show you it. The material has always been because it existed in God which is all and everything, omnipotent right? Omnipotent and omnipresent. So the material has always been but it began when it was perceived because that's when it became something. Before it was perceived it was just all. When we look out to these obstacles, all is all until we begin to start making things something, defining them, adding definition. Not adding real definition in the sense of making things but adding definition in our perception of it. Differentiating things, making distinctions, coming up with mythologies, imaginations, hallucinations, and projections. So now nothing or everything becomes many things. We are beginning the universe now with what we perceive. If I perceive a threat, that is the beginning of an experience of fear, right? If I perceive love, that is the beginning of the experience of joy for me. I'll give you an easy one, if I perceive things as gloomy, that is the beginning of the experience of sadness for me. Did sadness exist before I saw gloom? Did it? Did sadness exist before I perceived negativity? No, that was it's beginning for me because if I had perceived something else then happiness would have began for me. That would have been the beginning of happiness, the beginning of sadness, the beginning of joy, the beginning of excitement. When did it begin? It began at the moment that I perceived and defined things. It was not in my universe before then. So then if it wasn't in my universe which is the universe, I can assume that it didn't even exist. So we define and add dimension and emotion to the universe. When you break down the word emotion, we put 'energy into motion', that's emotions. It's all here but the emotion is the energy that puts it into motion whether its sadness, happiness, love, or peace, all of these things exist. That is the beginning of our universe. What am I saying? We are the perceivers. There is a material world; the space and the material that can be constructed to become any type of experience. All the material that we need can be constructed to have any experience that we decide to have, but it is void until we perceive it. When we perceive it, all the material we need to have that particular experience is available. Without our perception it has no meaning. When I say meaning because people ask 'What is the meaning or what is the purpose of life?' When I say meaning I mean that which colors it, not meaning in the sense of Webster's or The Oxford dictionary. But meaning can be what you feel. We don't realize that feeling is meaning. We ask people 'What does that mean to you?' They respond by saying 'I love it'. Because meaning is not always literate, scholastic definition, meaning that it's only just in the left brain, or in only one dimension of the brain. Meaning could be the feeling that you have for something in the sense of sentimental value, because certain things have sentimental value. People ask 'Well what does it mean?' You respond by saying 'It's sentimental'. You don't go into the dictionary to find out what your baby pictures mean do you? So the purpose of life or the meaning of life fits just as well into the context of emotion in terms of what you feel. That means a whole overall conceptualization of things not just in the sense of intellect. So we add meaning to things when we say 'I like this, I don't like that. I feel this way about this; I feel that way about that'. All that is meaning because since I feel that way about that, that means I don't want to experience that and if I feel happy about this thing that means I do want to experience that. So we create the meaning to all the material aspects of the universe. We give meaning to it. That's power. As conscious entities we give meaning without looking for meaning. Those looking for meaning believe in a mystery God, those who give meaning are in the driver's seat of their ship. Some of us are looking for meaning, 'what does this mean? It's 2012, what is this going to mean? The book of revelations what does it all mean? 144,000 what does it all mean?' Some of us are searching for meaning, whereas some of us are coming to know who we are and why we're here, what we feel, what we want to create and we are giving meaning. And how are we giving meaning? We are the energy accessed untapped to hold together what we choose to manifest. What we choose to manifest cannot subsist if we don't have the energy to hold it together, no matter what it is. Everything in the universe is scattering. Just as things are coming together everything in the universe is moving apart, so what's holding together what we want to create if things are moving apart as much as they are moving together? Our energy. The energy that we are putting forth perpetually to sustain is holding what we are doing together. If we want to hold it together stronger and if we want to hold more of it together then we need more energy. Back to my whole point in the beginning, we need to access more dynamic energy because where our energy falls short, it falls apart, bottom line. Your knees get weak, you fall. You've got a lot of energy in your legs and in your rootedness, you stand up. We've got to put more energy into our situation not desire to get and have more because having means sustaining and holding. Having also means maintaining but how are we maintaining what we have? What is the grand custodian of it all? The energy that you put forth because if you don't have the energy you cannot maintain it. If you want to drive a car and you haven't got any fuel it doesn't matter it's not going to move. You need the energy to move it around the city. Whatever we want requires us to have the energy to sustain its manifestation. We can't put more energy out, we're sad and we're depressed, we're up and we're down, we're down more than we're up, where's the energy to have this thing that we are talking about? We won't get the energy as long as we believe that there is a mythological reason why, 'it's not our energy, it's them, those and they.' I'm depressed 10 hours out the day, in a slump but I believe that I'm the one in a negative relationship not realizing I'm the negative person. I'm not even putting the energy out but I think I am getting over and I am right. But I don't even have the energy to sustain what it is I say I want and I use mythology; them, those, they, this or that circumstance as the reason why I'm on the couch. It's not that I don't have the energy to get up and I need to access the energy to infuse my life, and infuse my environment to contribute to the energetic paradigm of those that are around me to sustain the type of positive reality that I want to live in. But if reality is something objective based upon a mythological story you haven't got to deal with energy because energy makes you realize that you actually get only what you give. There's no story to that. There's no favor to go along with that. You say 'I want an extremely, positive, dynamic, exciting, fascinating, uplifting, elevating, joyful relationship. Now I said all that let me go sit down on the couch I'm tired.' Lol! 'Ooh I'm glad I got that out now let me go and relax'.

We cannot sustain the vibration of what we say we want to create and experience and what we are experiencing is at the level of vibration of the energy that we have mastered. So the positivity that we say we want in others and in the universe we can't have it unless we access the energy to vibrate, produce and be consistent with the force field of that which exists on that vibration. And that forces us to go beyond the negative attitude and to destroy mythologies about why we can't have the energy to create what we want. We want to deal with mythology and not deal with universal law. You can't lie with universal law; universal law is the reality of what is happening. Cause and effect, no story with it. 'Oh I don't like that about this person, I don't like this person doing this, I don't know why this person's doing that.' What's the cause? The energy that you're at is attracting that effect. You turn up the energy then you energize more and you attract what is at that energetic level. That's just the way the universe works. The law of vibration, the law of reciprocity, and the law of correspondence. But we get caught up in the stories and the soap operas and the soap operas are what people watch when they get lazy. For some of us, our lives have become a soap opera and we're sitting on the sofa just watching. And we don't want to exude the energy into the universe to create what we really want to experience so we sit on the sofa in our lives watching the dramatic and conflictual soap operas. Wow! The unfortunate thing is, if we want more we've got to be more. No matter what's going on in your life you cannot be happy longer than you can be happy, you cannot be excited longer than you can be excited, you cannot be joyful longer than you can be joyful. How do you expand your capacity to experience the joy that you want in your life? To my point, is it nutrition? Or is it changing your damn attitude, changing your perspective and having a paradigm shift? There are some people that are eating higher quality foods relatively in their own perception than we are and they're depressed. They're in Whole Foods thinking about going to the washroom and slitting their God damn wrists, lol! Literally, and hopefully the anti-oxidants and the pomegranate juice that they're drinking will save their life from their own negative thoughts. But if it does work it's because of the positive thoughts that they're able to channel about the pomegranate juice, drink it, internalize the thought energy of it and then think something else. We can drop a truckload of vegetables where there is so much damn kale that we can't even move around. We can juice all of it up and hook ourselves up to intravenous kale machines and we'd be just sitting on the damn couch. Until we access the dynamic energy, motivate and transform our consciousness, excel mentally at our over standing of our capacity to create, do, be and have more mentally. And go beyond the limits within one's own mind of what you are capable of doing, being and having as long as you have those limits nothing in the material world can get you past it. When you change the limits in your mind you have got past it in the material world without anything in the material world. If you have the limits in your mind then those limits are in the material world and there's nothing in the material world that can get you past it. It's a reality. But if you believe in the myth and remember that the myth is created at a low energy level. So the myth tells you that 'I need this, I need that, I need this, I need that' you get denser and denser and denser and then you can't even move. And your conscious vibration becomes so dense that you can't even see anything that you can use. So even though everything is there you still can't even see it. And that's when with people you say to them because you know that they've got all of these options and you project it to them and they keep saying 'I can't do anything, I can't do that, I can't' but you know and you're aware of the fact that they have millions of options but they cannot see it though they exist. They say 'well I've got to sell these drugs', 'I've got to do this', 'I've got to prostitute', 'I've got to do this'. You know that they have a million options but until they have a paradigm shift, that will be the totality of their experience. And that myth is their reality, and the myth is generated at a lower level of consciousness because when you get to a higher level of consciousness you'll begin to create a higher level story. It's a reality. We've got to go beyond our health fanaticism. Fanaticism is not health, health gives life. What gives us more life, more vitality, and more liveliness? Our mindset; us challenging ourselves to do more. There is no healthy way to eat; there is only a healthy way to be. You've got people that weigh 500 pounds and they're looking for a healthy way to eat. No, there's no healthy way to eat anymore at that point, there's a healthy way to be, where you are so happy it distracts you from eating. You've got so much dynamic energy to do and be and have what you want that you don't even have time to think about eating. You're so occupied, so satisfied, and self-fulfilled in manifesting your life purpose that you're not even thinking about anything to eat because you're fulfilled off of the spiritual quality of thought energy of achieving your goals and manifesting your highest vision. Man came to the universe to create the universe, that's the difference. Man came here to turn the material world into God's consciousness. The gerbil came here to eat seeds and nuts all day. Man came to create unfathomable, geometric, and geodesic figures and shapes. Man came to contemplate infinite possibility. Man came to outdo himself with every other next thought that he has. That is what separates him from the animals. Man must outdo himself with every other thing that he does. The horse hasn't got to do that, he's going to chew on the same grass he had yesterday that's the only thing he's got to do. Man must grow and develop his consciousness. He has to, he has to eat and gain a nutrition of an evolved mind. That's the difference between being alive and being mentally dead. Man is a self-sustained force and must project the energy in his own thoughts and in his own mind to sustain his existence. He cannot get that from food. Man cannot get that from food. If man does not out do himself he does not live. He gets bored and depressed and dies. Only in outdoing yourself and getting to higher levels of creativity and creative manifestation can you justify continually existing because you're constantly creating meaning. Man has to do that, nothing else has to do that. We must self-stimulate ourselves into animate existence. We have to. We're the only entity that must consciously self-sustain itself in order to exist. A monkey doesn't get depressed. He doesn't need it. He's happy with the same damn bananas he eats every day, no problem. If man does not develop consciously because he only exists differently from the animal world through conscious evolution, he's moving towards death. If we don't make our neurons fire and send electrical energy from source consciousness to manifest our physical selves, we perish. It's a reality. Our bodies operate because they receive electrical shocks from

God moment to moment. Every time I move a finger I've just received an electrical shock from God. If I stop sending shock waves from higher conscious dimensions from where I really exist into this physical body, it dies, it begins to atrophy. If I move and I'm able to amass supreme power through motion it's because those are the type of shocks that I'm sending from the electrical cosmic plane from where I really exist. We have to do this, send higher qualities of electrical energy of cosmic force into these bodies to evolve them into higher expressions of divine entities. We have to do this. We don't get that from food, it distracts us from doing that. We become denser and weightier, and now we have something so dense that the shocks can't even make it through it. Now you need more electricity to make it through more density to break it down, which we call metabolism. We need more energy to break through it because we have a disease; the disease of materialism where we get weighed down by the material world. The disease of materialism is that we become attached to so many things in the material world that we become weighed down, and by some of us getting weighed down we become more physically material, which results in us gaining weight. For others we become more mentally material where our thoughts are moving in slow motion. We have no inspiration; writer's block, no motivation. What is inspiration? Your-inner-spirit-in-action. That's what inspiration is. When your inner spirit cannot be animated into action in your body you have no inspiration; no in-spirit-in-action. It's something that we need from ourselves. And this isn't realizing that we are God, this isn't a self-realization, it's something that we need from ourselves to ascend, and to propel ourselves into this plane. There's something we need more from ourselves that we cannot get from here. We did not get ourselves from here, we didn't. Nothing that we ate gave us our self but we can project more of our self into this, thus we get more from ourselves and more out of this. They've got us addicted to capitalism; which is the belief in getting something outside of ourselves, making something outside of ourselves so more valuable than us. But if we had a million dollars to the roof in a room we wouldn't be able to even move. But this somehow is more valuable than us. The complete value of our existence however, is how much dynamic energy we can channel to move at accelerated speeds of creation. That's what's valuable. If you lose that I don't care how much money you've got, it doesn't matter because the dynamic energy of your existence is at a low level of vibration. And that's why they say 'health is wealth' but not just nutritional health, mental, spiritual and emotional health. You take somebody with a negative thought and put them on the best diet it's not gonna mean anything. They're gonna be a maniac with the best diet until they have a dynamic shift in their own consciousness. That's a reality. This is a very, very esoteric subject matter, very esoteric. Because it's making the individual really for a moment self-realize who they are and bring more of themselves to existence by being able to channel the energy of them into being without being distracted by the illusions of the material world. And that's work, because the material world has an inclination and it has a tendency to tell you who you are and you believe it. It has a tendency to do that, 'you're this', 'you can't do that', you know; 'you're limited to doing that', 'you can't do that', 'you can't have that', 'they never did that before', 'this is gonna happen if you do that' it has a tendency to give you limited ideas if that's what you're open to. When you go into meditation you're supposed to be open to higher consciousness so that you can receive thoughts about yourself on a higher plane. So that the thoughts about who you are come from the mind of God and not from the mind of man. A lot of us have got thoughts that came from the mind of man about what we're capable of and what's possible and we're looking for validation from the mind of man not from the mind of an infinite cosmic creator that is who we really are. That's the social validation thing. We're looking for man to tell us who we are and man is limited. Man will never do any more than he has already done but God consciousness will take man beyond anything that he has ever done. God consciousness will make man a liar. God consciousness will make everything man thinks he can do completely limited in the spectrum of what is possible. God consciousness will make man a liar and man will not become God until he can see the limits of his own thoughts and she will not become God until she can see the limits of her own thoughts. That's a reality. The limits of our thoughts make us less than Gods and make our experiences less than heavenly. Limited thought does this, when we accept a lesser thought and not continue to reach for the higher thought about things. We should stop and say 'Well let me reach for a higher thought about this' because if you want to get to a higher place you've got to grasp higher information and higher thoughts, but if you stop at the first level that you get to you will never get to a higher place. With every thought that comes up in your mind you should stop and say 'Well let me see if I can get a higher one than that.' Every situation and circumstance in your life, every thought that arises in you about it you should say 'Wait a minute, now let me stop there and let me see if I can get a higher thought than that'. The fool grasps on to whatever arises in his mind immediately, the fool grasps that and says 'That's the absolute truth I'm going with that'. The fool accepts the lowest of thoughts as the absolute reality leaving them stuck in experiences that they do not want to have because they can't think beyond it. Go to somebody and you say 'You don't need a job, you really don't need as much money as you think, you really don't even need a car.' You don't need anything that is going to make you a wage slave, that's what you're really saying.

Anything that's gonna make you a wage slave you don't need it. You know what the fool says? 'I don't believe you, I can't see that' because you can't think a higher thought. The fool cannot think higher. What makes him a fool? Not that he has lower thought, but the fact that he's not open to infinite possibility. That's what makes him a fool because to be honest all of our thoughts are relatively lower. Somebody could come to me with a higher thought and I could say to them 'Well you know; that really isn't possible, I couldn't, no I can't see that' you've just become a fool because you can't think beyond the spectrum of what you know to be true. You don't know that everything you think you know is ignorance based on the infinity of information and knowledge and that's a fool. There couldn't be any more to this universe than what you think you know and you're only using a small portion of your brain. And even though you can only see in one direction at a time, you couldn't possibly imagine that there's more to the universe than what you think you know, that's a fool. That's what you call closed-mindedness and the only slavery, the only prison for man is a closed mind. The only prison that man can ever be held in is a closed mind. The open minded will never be in prison they will always find a way and do you know why they'll find a way? Because if thought is infinite, if thought could be compiled in an infinite series of innumerable codes, only in our imagination can we find limit in the universe (whoa!). In any situation and circumstance only in our imagination can we find limitation. Because as long as you can keep thinking you can keep creating, and there is no limit to what your mind can create unless you close your damn mind and that's when immediately you go into prison. If we want something or anything, we don't have to have all the answers right now, we just have to open our mind to the possibility. Many say they want something but there mind is not open to the possibility. So even if there is a way to do it they will never experience it because their mind is not even open to the possibility of it happening. Their mind has already imagined and concluded that 'I have failed at that result' before even trying. They have concluded that 'I have already failed'. Even if they didn't have the answer or had not worked out the equation, fathoming the possibility is the beginning of the quest to an answer. It is a sincere beginning. Saying you're looking for an answer but your mind has concluded on defeat, that is an insincere beginning. 'I wanna know how to do this but I can't do that. Show me how to do it but I can't do it' that's an insincere start. We've got to open our minds to the possibilities of what can happen and live in there with no attachments, no mythologies, no history, and no knowledge! Just openness to possibility, how do you learn without openness to possibility? You can't learn you're faking. You can't learn where you believe that what you're seeking to learn is impossible. Giving up before you have even started. I'm challenging people. We've got to open up our minds up to the infinite possibilities of the universe. And we've really got to look at ourselves because we say that we want to change the world or change our lives but we don't realize that we must go beyond all negative thoughts and limited thoughts that enter into our atmosphere, no matter who it manifests in. So the co-dependent cult like group energy doesn't work because you've got to challenge negative and lower thoughts wherever they happen, whoever they happen to even if it's in you. Because you're navigating through the universal energy and you're bringing more energy to push through dense vibrations to experience the reality of what you know is possible. So we've got to constantly channel all negative and lower energy about what we can and cannot do and can and cannot have wherever and however it shows up. Because if we accept it wherever it shows up under any auspices or under any mythology then now we have created limits for ourselves. Why I am where I am at today is because I have kept moving through limits, limited thought forums, limited group circles, limited group minds about what we can achieve, be, do and have. I have kept gradually moving through it. People said 'we can't do this, we need this and that, that's not gonna work' I said let me keep it moving. I wasn't trying to create a group mind there or make that my eternal family. I wasn't trying to do that. I knew what my destiny was and I was moving towards my destiny aligning myself with those who could accelerate themselves to perceiving a great destiny for themselves. The group mind is dangerous because you are afraid to challenge a negative thought wherever it shows up for the sake of maintaining some type of group mind. You've got to challenge negative thoughts and I don't only mean in others but even in your own self because that takes us beyond the co-dependency of the group. 'We only need that to do that and we can't do that if we do that and I need this to do that' this is all limited thinking. There is no need in the universe. Any place or space where we are at can be used. This moment can be used to get us to where it is that we really want to be and go to. There is nothing that we need right now to get to where we want to be in life but the energy that lies inside of us. All the people with all the needs are in a state of illusion. They're saying 'I don't have everything in me right now to get to where it is that I wanna be in life.' If everything that you need does not exist in the now, how do you get there? The now is all that exists. If everything that you need does not exist, how do you get to there to get to more of what you need? You won't even make it. You won't make it until you realize that everything that you need you have now. That you don't need anything else, that you are everything, and that you are whole, perfect and complete.

6 THE RACE FOR WORLD CHANGE

We have used other people as excuses and we keep doing it. I say we are abusing the group mind. We use other people as excuses as to why we can't have and create what we want in our life when it is us that must move towards our destiny, that's our responsibility. We use other people as excuses 'people don't want to help us make progress, people down want to see world change, people don't listen' what if Marcus Garvey had said that? What if Gandhi had said that? Using other people to limit what our destiny is. We must embrace the destiny, we must grab our destiny by the helm ourselves and grip it and let it pull us into the future that we want for ourselves not holding onto anything else. We've got to get rid of these crutch relationships. They're crutches. We have created our own distractions in other people from manifesting our own destiny. We have done that as though somehow we are not the creators of our destiny and somehow we're limited to what someone else is doing when we're living off of our own heartbeat. So how the hell are we limited to what somebody else is doing if they're not stopping your heart? And they can only stop your heart because you're standing within striking distance, you're too damn close to em'! Or you're not animating enough damn energy to block them. None of these entities on the material plane is making our heart beat. Our energy is, our breathing is, and our projection of thought and if we project fear and doubt, we project a heart attack, and we stop it ourselves (lol!). We project a stroke by stressing ourselves out, we're creating this. We've got to grasp our destiny. And that doesn't separate us from anyone, that's not individualism but that's unity with those who are like minded and that want to create Heaven on Earth. I have unity with those who see the God in themselves. I'm unified with those that know that they have a right to manifest the most highest, positive, powerful and magnificent vision. I'm in unification with them. I'm already married, unified and connected with those and with their higher vibrational consciousness without attachment. Unified in mind, unified in principal, and unified in goals. Your goals unify you. If I'm going to California and you're going to Georgia we're not unified, and if we act like we're unified we're gonna snatch our arms apart because we're really moving in two different directions no matter what you call it. In our imagination or in an imagined-nation we're together, lol! But in reality we're not on the same vibration. But when you're on the same vibration you don't even have to look to see who's on the same vibration. You're running fast and you see who's running at the same speed that you are running at in the race, am I correct? All you've got to do is look forward and keep moving and when you look to the side they're running with you. If they're not running with you then they're not running at the same speed and they're not at the same place. You haven't got to worry about, judge or criticize people just God damn it run! Because criticizing and judging them is not going to make you win the race but depending on them will make you lose it. So we stop the criticism and judgment of others because that's distracting us from the finish line. Because we're looking back like 'you're not running, you're not running' and you don't see all the people passing you who aren't even paying any attention to you, they're just running. So it's not meant for judgment and criticism it's meant to accelerate ourselves into our own destiny. And you'll be surprised when you accelerate yourself and be radically honest and be radically clear and radically focused, you'll be surprised that some of the people that you thought weren't running fast will accelerate at some point in the race and be right there with you too. You thought that they fell off and that they weren't running at your speed but they were actually saying the same thing about you. And if everybody would just run, we would find out that we are all about to win the race together. Because being only one we are either going to win the race together or lose the race together, it's a reality. And that's what we do a lot of the time; we don't want to be the winner for everyone. We wanna stay focused on how others are losers. But if we focus on winning, everybody is a winner because with our example we show a winning image for everyone. We show the capabilities and the true possibilities of everyone and even though they lost they have won in you. Because even your victories represent theirs in the race for world change. So we've got to be all that we can be and this is not individualism. Make no apologies for your ability to maximize your highest potential given all situations and circumstances. Make no apologies for having the power to accelerate your life and move further towards achieving your goals in manifesting what you desire. You don't owe anyone an apology for that. And no one need not be judged or criticized because your destiny is further along for what you have to do and create than others. Embrace it and move forth within it, and when we embrace that the co-dependency is gone. I'm achieving the goals of self-realization for the people, they might not have got to that point in the race but it doesn't matter, I'm still winning it for them with no judgment or criticism about them or what they are, who they're with or what they're doing. I'm only focused on winning the race and that's the beauty about the race because when you win the race you win it for the human race. We've just got to focus on winning it. Some of us are running slow with people just to judge them, we're running at their speed just to tell them that they're not running fast. We're not winning by doing this because we should already be at the God damn finish line with what we're creating. So that's a good analogy. When no one will agree with you, agree with yourself about achieving your goals and your destiny. When everyone is tired, exhausted and unable to bring their energy out to be most productive, be your most productive. Win it for the human race. They will catch up if need be as is necessary but we are losing the race arguing and debating with them. We are losing the race. We have to put in the work now to manifest the vision that we have. Our vision is our own we must make this vision happen. Our vision is our baby it's our child, we can't neglect it or leave it with anybody else. That doesn't mean we don't love other people and we don't have compassion for others but we cannot leave this baby (this vision) with them. We don't know if they're going to take care of it like it needs to be taken care of. That's why it was given to us. Our vision was born through us and born to us to manifest. And it is the most mature and adult thing to do, to take responsibility to bring them into reality with no excuses and no apologies. Our vision is depending on us to live and we're depending on it to live. If it doesn't live we don't live because we can only live through it. And if we don't create it we have no life at all. We just have matter and matter is not life. Matter becomes life when you take a rock and sculpt it into a sculpture. Then you see life. Then you also see life imitating art and you see art imitating life. But without that It's just matter. And anything that's just matter doesn't matter. That's a reality.

7 CLARITY

If we have a vision in our third eye we better get clear on it and step into it or it's never going to happen. The universe doesn't owe us anything, nothing is going to give us nothing, there will be no stroke of luck or chance, either you're going to get clear, focused and produce it or it's NOT going to happen. That doesn't sound too optimistic does it? But it's true, it isn't going to happen, the universe is not going to do it for us but it will meet us halfway. That's the law of cause and effect; halfway. You put this much out you get that much back; the universe will meet us halfway. We've got to get clear. And the majority of the problems, circumstances and wasted energies, the majority of the negative situations in our lives is because we are not clear. When we get clear the fuzziness goes away. If we get clear the negative situations are over with. How do clear people argue? If I'm clear that ghosts don't exist how long am I gonna argue with you about it? I'm absolutely clear that there are no ghosts and that there is no Boogieman in the closet, how long am I going to sit and argue with somebody about it? To the degree that we spend time arguing we are not clear. And that's when we need to shut up and get clear. Get clear! And when we get clear we will see the need not to argue. The need to argue will become less. Clear people don't argue, they make solid intellectual points and leave it. If we're arguing, we are not clear because whatever you're clear about it would be stupid, it would be absolutely stupid to argue, am I correct? If I had a cup which was full of water and somebody told me that it wasn't how long am I gonna spend arguing with them? I'm absolutely clear that there's something in the cup I'm like 'well OK, get your medication. ' Clear people don't argue, insane people argue. You're clear about your life destiny, you're in the driver's seat, what are you arguing about? We argue because we want power and control. You are power and you are control. You were born that. That's what you are. We all are. Being deluded to that reality we come to the illusion that someone has some power and control outside of us. You know the ones that have it? The ones that we give it to. That's it. And do you know how we give it to them? By interfacing with them based on the illusion that it is true. If you knew you were free why are you arguing about freedom? You don't know that you're free that's the problem. The argument is in your own mind. So you attract somebody to argue about it with. Until you wake up and realize and say that 'wait a minute, I am. What am I arguing about? I am free' we will continue to attract these situations and circumstances to us out of our lack of clarity. We must be absolutely clear about what we're creating and if we're not clear in moments, we've got to stop and say 'What am I actually and really creating?' Because no God or Goddess is going to create arguments. They make solid points. They navigate through experiences; they don't stop in tornadoes do they? They don't drive up to earthquakes and park their car; they navigate through friction and resistance to the point of where they are going. Our arguments last too long. We must make clear, explosive, dynamic points, statements and move forward. Those people have power. I read a book, which said that the wealthiest people in the world can make a decision in 15 seconds. If you're arguing you're not decisive. Whose fault is that, that you're not decisive about what you're creating? The person you're arguing with? 'I don't know what the hell I'm creating and it's your fault. I don't know what the hell I wanna do and it's your fault'. You've got to shut up and get clear and then you'll realize that there's no argument. That's schizophrenia projecting itself as two different people with schizophrenia. You get two people together that are bi-polar you get an argument. You get one person that's clear there is no argument. It takes two unclear people to argue, if either one of them gets clear, the arguments over with, am I right? It's over with. Somebody says 'Did you put that there?' 'I know I didn't put that there' I'm gone. If I'm unsure and unclear of what I did and my memory is bad 'I didn't put that there, well maybe, no I didn't because I didn't do that and I didn't', there's a lack of clarity there isn't there? If you have doubt about yourself, and doubt how you're perceived by others there's a lot of room for arguments isn't there? I doubt that I'm a good person I have to argue about whether I'm right or wrong or whether what I'm doing is right. I'm not clear about it. And in the argument I'm trying to convince myself about myself. I just have projected the counter thoughts about myself as somebody else. Clear people make solid decisions and move forward closer towards their destiny. That's what they do. Unclear people stay in dense vibrations and hope and pray to a mystery God that circumstances change. Clear people get to work on manifesting their destiny. Unclear people pray that luck, divination, astrology, numerology, and even nutrition will change their life. But it doesn't, they stay in the same messed up condition with a better diet, with another astrology reading, with some more numbers to add up; numerology, with different terra cards but in the same messed up situation. We were arguing with stakes now we're arguing with avocadoes. We were mad as hell with pork now we're mad as hell with vegetable drinks. What's the difference? Do the spiritual work. There is no escape from it. Use vitamin self. We've got to do the spiritual work for real and when the work is complete there is a better decisive, stronger, clearer and focused person that no longer argues but adds and projects harmony and clarity into the lives of others. That means after someone experiences you, they're clearer about who they are and what they want to do. Because clarity gives birth to what? Clarity and confusion gives birth to what? Confusion. If the people around you are confused it's because you are not clear, because clarity gives birth to clarity. If you are clear other people can't help but to be clear, because you are the line that they can measure themselves against. They can measure themselves against what is real for you and from that they see automatically what is real for them. If you are unclear, they are unclear, everybody is unclear. When somebody gets clear everybody gets clear. It's just the way it works, 100%. Everybody is waiting on everybody else to get clear; co-dependency. People may say 'How can you say 'I am God', why can't you say 'we are God?'' because you know what? I can only be clear for one person. But if I'm clear 'I am God' I know others are clear that they can be God too, because the clarity is there. I'm not going to argue for nobody that 'we are God'. You could win that argument 'No I'm not!' But you can't win an argument that 'I am God' do you know why? Because I wouldn't even argue it. Because I say it affirmatively, and in projecting and manifesting God people that can identify with the divine example that is being set will move into being God themselves. If I said 'we are' that's weak because the 'we' doesn't make 'I' but 'I' makes 'we'. The 'I' is not made up of 'we' but the 'we' is made up of 'Is'. So when I say 'I am' those who identify with it I am saying 'we are'. Those who do not identify with it I am saying 'you're not'. It's the law of polarity and the law of duality. I do something great people see their greatness. I don't sit back and say 'they're great'. I demonstrate greatness they identify with it as a reality. That's how it should be. We sit and talk and say others are great. You know what makes greatness real? We demonstrate it not just say other people are. We are not going to get greatness in the universe by just going around saying that other people are great. We get it by demonstrating greatness in our lifestyle, in our way of life, in obtaining our goals and going beyond our limitations and the challenges in our lives. We are showing the reality of greatness versus sitting back saying 'we, we, we, we, we' but 'we' aren't doing anything. Show it! Make greatness manifest and known in this universe through your actions. And people will hop onto that and imitate it like the hundred monkey syndrome and emulate it and model themselves after it. And if you say it hard enough they can't help but to hear it as them. That's just the way that the mind works because you've changed the field of thought, the psychic field of thoughts and they accept the thought. When you say 'I am great' all they hear in themselves is 'I am great'. They forget that it's you saying it and all they hear is 'Wait, I am great' because they can't help but to. If it's spoken long and strong and loud and proud enough then they hear the 'I am' echoing from deep within their own existence even though it was said outside of them. Because when you hear something your mind repeats it as though you said it if it's spoken hard enough. Whatever you comprehend and interpret you own. If you truly comprehend it, it has become a part of you and your understanding. So we don't go around talking, we demonstrate the 'I', the 'I' and 'I'. So take time and be clear, and be decisive. We can be quiet and silent until we are clear. We don't have to jump on vibrations of confusion. We can just wait until we're clear. Speak then. I don't speak until I'm clear, I haven't got anything to say until when I open my mouth I am absolutely clear. What else do I have to say other than confusion but clarity? There's no middle ground, either I'm saying something absolutely clear or I'm speaking confusion. So until I can say something absolutely clear I have absolutely nothing to say. Anything else is just a good argument. And I'm not writing this book to present good arguments I'm writing this book to speak the truth into existence. And if every individual after reading this book all they can say is that 'I'm even absolutely more clear, I'm clearer' my job is done. And what we should be, do and have should make other people clearer about who they are. Not just a movement, not just trying to reach people but presenting something to them in a form of ourselves in what we're manifesting that makes them more clear about who they are by contrasting their experiences. After they see what we're doing they can't be anything but clear about who they are automatically. 'Wow! We can do that'. Not us begging and trying to convince them, just show and prove. We've got to show and prove in our clarity, in our decisiveness and what we manifest on this planet. Others must become absolutely clear. When they come into our space they should be clear. Even if they don't step into the clarity, even if they don't embrace it in the exact same way that we do, at least they are clear. That's our goal. You forget about everyone else until you see your own divinity to the point where you're seeing your own divinity in everyone else. Forget about everyone else, the myths and the stories, until all you see and are aware of is your own divinity to the point that that's all you can see in everybody else. Wow! You don't see dramas and roles of antagonism, struggles or battles; you don't see any of that. You just see the divinity in your own self as you are propelling yourself forward into the future in all and in every situation and circumstance in your life. How can you be mad or upset with that type of attitude? If we're upset and mad all throughout the day, what's the problem? Our attitude. Because if you can be made upset that's a flaw in you because your approach to the experiences that you have in life is inferior, and an inferior approach leads to an upset person. It's an inferior approach; you've got to accept it for what it is. Because the anger in them does not solve the problem. Right action solves the problem. Clear thought and clear mindedness solves the problem. So the superior approach is to become absolutely clear on the solution not reacting to the problem. We have to get to a point of a superior mind and a superior approach to things going on in our lives if we want superior results.

8 BE THE SAVIOR

So ending in talking about the health fanaticism, I quote the Honorable Elijah Muhammad when I say 'we're not here to live to eat' or eat to live really. Eating is not life, creating is life. And when you create life at the essence of your consciousness then you can create what you want to eat. The food that you want to eat can be manifested. But it can't be manifested if you're trying to create from the food that you feel like you need to eat that is not there. You can't create from that. You can create from where you are from and when you put more energy out into the universe there will be more of anything that you want or need. Even things that you don't have categories for, things that you're not even conscious of that is important to you, when you put more energy out, all of it will start showing up. Don't put out the energy of want; don't put out the energy of desire, put out the energy of self, which is putting more of your own power into the universe, and more of the force of your spirit into the universe. That's what we all need to be doing not just sitting around wanting things and not having enough of things. We need to put our energy forth and then put out more, and then more will just start showing up. More of any and everything will show up. It's a reality. Like if you don't worry about money but you work five jobs you put the energy out to work five jobs and somehow you automatically have stuff to buy the things you need. A job is a terrible example but the reality is putting out more energy into the universe and watching more manifest. Putting out more energy is not sitting around being depressed in fear, lack, doubt, limitation and in want. Putting out more energy is moving into putting out more dynamic force, which is more positive attitude synergizing. We say we want to give something to people, give positive energy to people. That puts the universe in motion because that's creating positive emotion and while you put positive emotion out they have all the material, so they just give the material to you because they've got it already. They need positive energy in motion. What I'm telling you is that your wealth is your energy that you transfer to others. And if your attitude is negative you have no wealth of energy to give to anyone to receive anything that's worth anything. If all we do is talk to people and we don't have positive encouragement for them, we talk to them and all we've got for them is our problems, what are we giving? We're vampires. But if we give positive energy versus dwelling on our problems and raping the universe then we will get more of what we want from the universe automatically. If we take from the universe through negative attitudes and negative vibrations we will lose even what the hell we have. We will become nothing. People come to you and say 'I have something positive that I want to give to you, I have something positive that I want to share with you', you say 'Hold up, let me tell you all of my problems' By the time you get through they have forgotten what they had to give. We've got to get extremely positive. We have to become extremely happy and extremely encouraging to others. You know what I mean by that? We have to get to a positive level of energetic transference. We have to stop being victims and start giving victory to others. And they'll give it back to us. We have become too obsessed with being victims of somebody else, of myths, of what somebody else is doing or not doing or did to us. We've got to stop becoming victims and start giving the victory to ourselves. Where we're playing the victim is where we need to play the savior, because two victims cannot help each other. Who's going to be the savior? This is homework! Situations where you play the victim at in your life challenge yourself to be the savior right there. And save the person that you feel has victimized you. Be the savior for the person that you feel victimized you because two victims is a pity party. Somebody's got to be the savior. To be the manifestation of God and to be God in person is to become our own savior. Realize the energy is us. Be clear within ourselves. Don't give ourselves any excuse not to manifest and bring forth the highest energy that is inside of us irregardless of people, situations, persons, conditions and things. Go beyond all of them, that's being transcendental. Go beyond all situations and circumstances and bring the highest out of yourself no matter what. Use no situation, person, place, condition, thing, or scenario, as an excuse not to bring the higher out of yourself irregardless. Destroy the mythologies, the stories, the victimizations and bring a higher form and higher quality of energy from your own being and from your own existence and watch your life transform before your very own eyes.

CPSIA information can be obtained at www.ICGtesting.com
Printed in the USA
BVOW071437040313

314682BV00001B/207/P